HOW RELIABLE ARE THE GOSPELS?

The Synoptic Gospels in the Ancient Church: The Testimony to the Priority of the Gospel of Matthew

F. David Farnell

Copyright © 2018 F. David Farnell

All rights reserved. Except for brief quotations in articles, other publications, book reviews, and blogs, no part of this book may be reproduced in any manner without prior written permission from the publishers. For information, write, support@christianpublishers.org

Unless otherwise stated, Scripture quotations are from the Updated American Standard Version (UASV) Copyright © 2018 by Christian Publishing House

HOW RELIABLE ARE THE GOSPELS? The Synoptic Gospels in the Ancient Church: The Testimony to the Priority of the Gospel of Matthew

Authored by F. David Farnell

ISBN-13: **978-1-949586-65-7**

ISBN-10: **1-949586-65-0**

THE SYNOPTIC GOSPELS: The Testimony to the Priority of the Gospel of Matthew 1

Bibliography 49

THE SYNOPTIC GOSPELS: The Testimony to the Priority of the Gospel of Matthew

Introduction[1]

The Gospel of Matthew was the church's most popular Gospel in the decades up to the time of Irenaeus (ca. A.D. 180). After an extensive analysis of Matthew's influence on early Christianity, Massaux relates,

> Of all the New Testament Writings, the Gospel of Mt. was the one whose literary influence was the most widespread and the most profound in Christian literature that extended into the last decades of the second century. . . .
>
> Until the end of the second century, the first gospel remained the gospel par excellence . . . .
>
> The Gospel was, therefore, the normative fact of Christian life. It created the background for ordinary Christianity.[2]

Moreover, the unanimous and unquestioned consensus of the Church Fathers was that Matthew was the first gospel written, and almost without exception, the early church placed the Gospel of Matthew first in the

---

[1] This appeared in the Master's Seminary Journal, vol 10/1 (Spring 1999) 53-86 as a Festschrift for Robert L. Thomas.

[2] Édouard Massaux, *The Influence of the Gospel of Saint Matthew on Christian Literature Before Saint Irenaeus*, trans. by Norman J. Belval and Suzanne Hecht, Arthur J. Bellinzoni, ed., 3 vols. (Macon, Ga.: Mercer University, 1993), 3:186-87.

canon of the New Testament. Petrie observes, "Until the latter half of the eighteenth century, the apostolic authorship of 'the Gospel according to Matthew' seems to have been generally accepted."[3]

However, the Enlightenment and its spawning of historical-critical methodologies—particularly that aspect of the system called "Source Criticism"—marked the beginning of the end of that viewpoint.[4] Most New Testament scholars at the turn of the twenty-first century resoundingly reject the unanimous testimony of the early church regarding Matthean priority in favor of the Two- or Four-Source Theory[5] of how the Synoptic Gospels came into existence.[6] That rejection characterizes not only those of a liberal-theological perspective. It also extends to include many who probably would classify themselves as

---

[3] C. Steward Petrie, "The Authorship of 'The Gospel According to Matthew': A Reconsideration of the External Evidence," *New Testament Studies* 14 (1967-1968): 15. Stonehouse, a leading advocate of Markan priority, admitted, "[T]he tradition concerning the apostolic authorship of Matthew is as strong, clear, and consistent and . . . the arguments advanced against its reliability are by no means decisive . . . the apostolic authorship of Matthew is as strongly attested as any fact of ancient church history" (Ned B. Stonehouse, *The Origins of the Synoptic Gospels* [Grand Rapids: Eerdmans, 1963], 46-47, cf. 76-77).

[4] Bernard Orchard and Harold Riley, *The Order of the Synoptics, Why Three Synoptic Gospels?* (Macon, Ga.: Mercer, 1987), 111.

[5] The Two-Source Theory contends that Mark was written first, then Matthew and Luke wrote in dependence on Mark and a document called "Q," which contained material common to Matthew and Luke but not found in Mark. The Four-Source Theory adds documents called "M"—used by Matthew in addition to the others—and "L"—used by Luke in addition to the others.

[6] See Bernard Orchard and Thomas R. W. Longstaff, *J. J. Griesbach: Synoptic and text-critical studies 1776-1976* (Cambridge: Cambridge University, 1978), 134; William R. Farmer, *The Synoptic Problem* (Macon, Ga.: Mercer University, 1976), 48-49; Burnett Hillman Streeter, *The Four Gospels, A Study of Origins* (Macmillan and Co., 1924), 151-98. Orchard and Longstaff cite Griesbach as an example of one who criticized the early fathers. Farmer cites the lack of evidence supporting the Two- (or Four-Source) Theory.

conservative evangelicals, men such as Hill, Carson along with Moo and Morris, Martin, and France who explain away the evidence from Papias and church tradition regarding Matthean priority in deference to a theory of modern vintage that requires the priority of Mark.[7] Few conservative evangelicals today dare to challenge the "findings" of Source Criticism.

The theory of Mark's being written first flies in the face of what is quite clear from the writings in the early church, as Massaux has pointedly demonstrated:

> The literary influence of the Gospel of Mk. is practically nil of these writings [i.e., the church writings of the first two centuries up to Irenaeus]. This characteristic of the early tradition constitutes a strange phenomenon. How can we explain this silence of tradition, if, as is generally believed, Mk. was the first of the canonical gospels? How can we explain the first Christians hardly resorted to it, so that it appeared almost nonexistent? Did it not respond, perhaps to the exigencies and concrete needs of the community of the time? Or have we been wrong to elevate it to the detriment of the Gospel of Mt.?[8]

Someone besides Massaux needs to set the record straight. The church fathers must have their hearing, apart from a dogmatism that bases itself on a late-blooming theory regarding gospel sequence. They lived much closer

---

[7] David Hill, *The Gospel of Matthew*, in The New Century Bible Commentary (Grand Rapids: Eerdmans, 1972), 28; D. A. Carson, Douglas J. Moo, and Leon Morris, *An Introduction to the New Testament* (Grand Rapids: Zondervan, 1992), 70-71; R. T. France, *Matthew*, Tyndale New Testament Commentary (Grand Rapids: Eerdmans, 1985), 34-38; Ralph P. Martin, *New Testament Foundations*, vol. 1 of *The Four Gospels* (Grand Rapids: Eerdmans, 1975), 139-60, 225.

[8] Massaux, *Gospel of Saint Matthew*, 3:188.

to the composition of the gospels than anyone associated with the Enlightenment. Also, they were scholars in their own right, so it is a grave mistake to dismiss their testimony so casually as moderns have tended to do. They bear a unified testimony against critical assumptions of the last two centuries that have supported the priority of Mark and the associated Two- (or Four-) Source Theory. The discussion of their writings will also evidence the shortcomings of the avenue of Source Criticism that results in the Two-Gospel Theory.[9]

Papias

Early in the first half of the second century A.D., Papias was bishop of Hierapolis in the Phrygian region of the province of Asia—a city about 20 miles west of Colosse and 6 miles east of Laodicea.[10] Nothing much is known of Papias's life beyond the comment of Irenaeus that he was "one of the ancients" (ἀρχαῖος ἀνήρ, *archaios aner*).[11] His writing activity dates between ca. A.D. 95 and 110.[12] That

---

[9] The Two-Gospel Theory holds that Matthew was written first, then Luke wrote depending on Matthew, and finally Mark wrote in dependence on Matthew and Luke.

[10] See Eusebius *Ecclesiastical History* 3.36.1-2.

[11] Irenaeus *Against Heresies* 5.33.3-4; cf. Eusebius *Ecclesiastical History* 3.39.1-2.

[12] Yarbrough gives five convincing arguments supporting this date: First, Papias's position in Eusebius's *Ecclesiastical History* (Book 3) places him with young Polycarp, Ignatius and even Clement, i.e. those who were the immediate successors to the apostles. Moreover, in Book 3 Eusebius catalogues no matters later than Trajan's reign (97-117), and Book 4 opens with the twelfth year of Trajan (ca. 109), indicating that Eusebius viewed Papias as flourishing before A.D. 109. Second, Eusebius's Chronicon places the aged Apostle John, Papias, Polycarp and Ignatius (in that order) in the same entry with the year "100" placed next to this entry as part of his running table of dates [see Helm, *Die Chronik des Hieronymus*, 7:193-194]; Third, Irenaeus called Papias "one of the ancients" (ajrcai'o" ajnhvr-Irenaeus *Against Heresies* 5.33.3-4; cf. Eusebius *Ecclesiastical History* 3.39.1-2). Since Irenaeus most likely had personal

early dating makes his works crucial, for he is one of only a few witnesses to a very early period of church history.

Papias (along with his friend and contemporary, Polycarp) was a disciple and personal acquaintance of the Apostle John because Irenaeus wrote that Papias was "the hearer of John."[13] Unfortunately, Papias's writings are no longer extant. Only fragments of his works remain and

---

contact with Polycarp, who was a companion of Papias (Eusebius *Ecclesiastical History* 5.20.4-8; Irenaeus *Against Heresies* 5.33.4; cf. Eusebius *Ecclesiastical History* 3.39.1), he is not liable to be mistaken in his opinion of Papias's connections with earliest apostolic origins. Fourth, Irenaeus confirms that Papias was a hearer of John (Eusebius *Ecclesiastical History* 3.39.1). Fifth, neither Eusebius nor Irenaeus identifies Papias as an anto-gnostic witness, thus placing Papias much earlier than such gnostics as Valentinus, Basilides and Marcion. whose teachings both Irenaeus and Eusebius were trying to refute. See Yarbrough, "The Date of Papias," 186-187. For a more complete review of the strong evidence linking Papias to the date of ca. 95-110, see Robert W. Yarbrough, "The Date of Papias: A Reassessment," *Journal of the Evangelical Theological Society* 26 (June 1983): 181-91; Robert H. Gundry, *Matthew, A Commentary on His Handbook for a Mixed Church Under Persecution*, 2nd ed. (Grand Rapids: Eerdmans, 1994), 611-13.

[13] See Irenaeus *Against Heresies* 5.33.4; also quoted by Eusebius *Ecclesiastical History* 3.39.1. Regarding Eusebius' skeptical attitude about whether Paplas ever heard the apostle John (*Ecclesiastical History* 3.39.1-2) see William R. Schoedel, *Polycarp, Martyrdom of Polycarp, Fragments of Papias*, vol. 5 of *The Apostolic Fathers*, Robert M. Grant, ed. (Camden, N. J.: Thomas Nelson, 1967), 89-92; Rudolf Helm, *Eusebius Werke*, vol. VII of *Die Chronik des Hieronymus*, in Die Griechischen Christlichen Schriftsteller der Ersten Jahrunderte (Akademie-Verlag: Berlin, 1956): 193-94; 412-13. For persuasive evidence that Papias *did* have direct contact with the apostle, see Robert H. Gundry, *Matthew, A Commentary on His Handbook for a Mixed Church under Persecution*, 2nd ed. (Grand Rapids: Eerdmans, 1994), 611-613. Eusebius' skepticism may have stemmed from his anti-chiliastic view as opposed to that of Papias (and Irenaeus) who strongly affirmed a physical reality of the millennium (see Eusebius, *Ecclesiastical History* 3.39.12-13). Or, it may have resulted from Papias' alleged preference for oral tradition rather than authorized books as his sources (see Eusebius, *Ecclesiastical History* 3.39.4; cf. also Robert M. Grant, ed., "An Introduction," in vol. 1 of *The Apostolic Fathers, A New Translation and Commentary* [New York: Thomas Nelson and Sons, 1964], 86).

are largely known through quotations by later Fathers, especially Eusebius. Papias wrote a series of five treatises entitled *Interpretation of the Oracles of the Lord* (Λογίων κυριακῶν ἐξηγήσεως, *logiōn kuriakōn exēgēseōs*) in which he draws information from the remaining, living-eyewitness sources, i.e., the Apostle John himself and another original disciple of Jesus named Ariston, concerning what the apostles had said or done.[14] In essence, Papias's assertions had their foundation in direct "eyewitness" (i.e., firsthand) reports.[15] If Papias wrote ca. A.D. 95-110, then the information that he imparts reaches well back into the first century and is an invaluable source of information regarding the gospels.

Papias included a brief account in his *Expositions* regarding the composition of Matthew: "**Matthew collected** (συνετάξατο, *sunetaxato*) **the oracles** (τὰ λόγια, *ta logia*) **in the Hebrew language** (Ἑβραΐδι διαλέκτῳ, *Hebraidi dialektōi*) **and each interpreted them** (ἡρμήνευσεν, *hērmēneusen*) **as best he could.**"[16] (bold

---

[14] Eusebius denied that Papias was a direct hearer of the Apostle John by inferring that another John, John the Elder who was different from John the Apostle, lived in Ephesus at the time (*Ecclesiastical History* 3.39.5-6). A close reading of Papias's words, however, reveals that he neither affirmed nor denied that he was hearer or eyewitness of the apostles. He does not mention it in the passage. Petrie argues, "[T]here is nothing to justify the careless confidence with which Eusebius contradicts Irenaeus" (C. Stewart Petrie, "Authorship of 'The Gospel According to Matthew'," 15-32 [esp. 17-18]). Furthermore, even if Papias was not a personal disciple of John, as Lightfoot contended, "still his age and country place him in more or less close connection with the traditions of the Apostles; and it is this fact which gives importance to his position and teaching" (J. B. Lightfoot, *Essays on the Work Entitled Supernatural Religion* [London: Macmillan and Co., 1889], 142).

[15] Eusebius *Ecclesiastical History* 3.39.15-16. Papias's statement regarding John the disciple and the Elder John probably referred to one and the same person, i.e. John the Apostle (Petrie, "Authorship," 18-24; Gundry, *Matthew*, 611-13).

[16] Eusebius *Ecclesiastical History* 3.39.16. All quotes of Papias and Eusebius in Part 1 of this chapter are taken from the Loeb Classical Library

publisher) A great deal of conflict, however, has raged around this short statement, especially regarding the meaning and significance of the words "the oracles" (*ta logia*) and the phrase "in the Hebrew language" (*Hebraidi dialektōi*). An understanding of the latter expression has some impact on how one interprets the former.

Ta logia *as an independent collection of Jesus' sayings.* Regarding the meaning of "the oracles" (*ta logia*), Scholars exhibit several major interpretations. Some think that it refers to an independent collection of Jesus' sayings, perhaps Q.[17] T. W. Manson popularized the view:

> In Eusebius we find a quotation from Papias stating that "Matthew composed the oracles (*ta logia*) in the Hebrew language, and each one interpreted them as he was able." This obviously cannot refer to the first Gospel, which is essentially a Greek work based on Greek sources, of which Mark is one. It is, however, possible that what is meant is the document which we now call Q.[18]

Adding support to this conclusion was the fact that *ta logia* is not the usual way of referring to a "gospel" and would be rather unique, for the normal descriptive term already seen by the time of Papias and evidenced in early

---

Series. See Eusebius, *The Ecclesiastical History*, with an English translation by Kirsopp Lake, 2 vols. (London: William Heinemann, 1926).

[17] According to most, the designation "Q" stands for the first letter of the German word for "source," *Quelle*. That position, however, is debated. See the discussion in John J. Schmitt, "In Search of the Origin of the Siglum Q," *Journal of Biblical Literature* 100 (1981): 609-11.

[18] T. W. Manson, *The Teaching of Jesus* (London: SCM Press, 1957), 18-20; cf. also *idem*, *The Sayings of Jesus* (London: SCM Press, 1949), 18-19; *idem*, "The Gospel of Matthew," in *Studies in the Gospels and Epistles*, Matthew Black, ed. (Manchester: Manchester University, 1962), 82-83.

manuscripts of the gospels would be το εὐαγγελιον (*to euaggelion*, "the gospel").[19]

That explanation of *ta logia*, however, is dubious for several reasons. First, Papias does not use *ta logia* to refer only to sayings but also to the deeds of Jesus. The title of Papias' work, *Interpretation of the Oracles of the Lord* (Λογίων κυριακῶν ἐξηγήσεως, logiōn kuriakōn exēgēseōs) implies that more than Jesus' words are encompassed in its meaning, for enough is known regarding this work that he did not restrict it in scope to an exposition merely of Jesus's words.[20]

Second, in Eusebius's *Ecclesiastical History* 3.39.15-16, Papias commented that in composing his gospel, Mark, being Peter's interpreter, "wrote accurately all that he remembered . . . of the things said *or done* by the Lord" [emphasis added] and immediately after this spoke of Peter as "not making, as it were, an arrangement of the Lord's oracles (σύνταξιν τῶν κυριακῶν ποιούμενος λογίων, *suntaxin tōn kuriakōn poioumenos logiōn*), so that Mark did nothing wrong in thus writing down single points as he remembered them." Since Mark's gospel included deeds as well as words, the expression τῶν. . . λογίων (*tōn . . . logiōn*, "the oracles") must include both too.

Third, the parallelism between these two phrases— "the things said or done" (τά ... ἢ λεχθέντα ἢ πραχθέντα, τά ... ē *lechthenta* ē *prachthenta*) and "the oracles of the Lord" (τῶν κυριακῶν ... λογίων, tōn kuriakōn ... logiōn)— in immediate juxtaposition demonstrates that the latter expression, i.e. "the oracles of the Lord" (i.e. tōn kuriakōn

---

[19] Lampe cites only two examples of this phrase referring to "the gospels" contained in the *Chronicon Paschale* (seventh century A.D.) (see "lovgion, tov" in G. W. H. Lampe, *A Patristric Greek Lexicon* (Oxford: At the Clarendon, 1961), 806.

[20] Eusebius *Ecclesiastical History* 3.39.1.

8

... logiōn), can encompass both the deeds as well as the words of Jesus.

Fourth, immediately after these statements regarding Mark's gospel, Papias applies the term ta logia to Matthew's work, thus making it hard to avoid the conclusion that he refers to Matthew's gospel rather than some hypothetical sayings source like Q.[21] Therefore, the ta logia is most naturally understood as a synonym for the gospel.[22]

No evidence exists that such a document as "Q" ever existed at Papias' time or any other time. The increasing skepticism of a wide spectrum of NT scholars regarding the nature (e.g., make-up and extent) of Q and whether such a document ever really existed in church history make this suggestion highly dubious.[23]

---

[21] Kittel argues that Papias' use of the term lovgia (logia) cannot be confined to mere sayings or collections of sayings, but more likely has reference to the whole gospel, i.e., words and deeds of Jesus: "[I]t is just as clear and indisputable that in the light of the usage of the LXX, NT and early Church the more comprehensive meaning is also possible" Gerhard Kittel, "lovgion," *TDNT*, 4:141.

[22] See Lightfoot, *Essays on Supernatural Religion*, 172-76.

[23] See Stewart Petrie, "Q is Only What You Make It," *Novum Testamentum* 3 (1959): 28-33. Petrie points out that the wide variety and conflicting hypotheses concerning the nature and extent of Q have cast great suspicion on the validity of the hypothesis for its existence. Farrar, though holding to the idea that Matthew and Luke utilized Mark, nonetheless, argues that against the existence of Q (A. M. Farrar, "On Dispensing with Q," in *Studies in the Gospels*, Essays in Memory of R. H. Lightfoot, D. E. Nineham, ed. [Oxford: Blackwell, 1955]: 55-88). After an extensive analysis, Linnemann, a former post-Bultmannian who at one time was a staunch advocate of the Two-Source Hypothesis, concludes that any idea of Q is a "fantasy, is "based in error," and "proves untenable" (Eta Linnemann, "Gospel of Q," *Bible Review* XI [August 1995]: 19-23, 42-43).

Ta logia as a collection of OT proof texts.

A second view similar to the first is that ta logia refers to an OT *testimonia* collection (i.e., a book of OT proof texts) compiled by Matthew from the Hebrew canon for use in Christian apologetics, one that eventually was incorporated into canonical Matthew. Hunt forcefully argues,

> [Λ]όγια has nothing to do with the title of any book, but is a technical term meaning O.T. oracles. That is to say that λόγια was not the *name* of a book composed by St. Matthew, or by anyone else, but was a description of the contents of the book; it was composed of λovgia, which had been arranged by St. Matthew.[24]

For Hunt, those who would see the term λovgia as meaning "gospel" most likely "have been hypnotized by tradition" and "for whatever τa; λovgia may have been taken as meaning at a later period, it could not have meant *The Gospel according to St. Matthew* when originally written; since nobody will maintain that a gospel was ever called τὰ λόγια."[25] Similarly, Grant asserts that that τῶν κυριακῶν ... λογίων predominately refer to "divine utterances" like those contained in the OT.[26] Therefore, Papias seems to refer to Matthew's collection of OT

---

[24] B. P. W. Stather Hunt, *Primitive Gospel Sources* (London: James Clarke & Co., 1951), 184; cf. also Rendel Harris, *Testimonies*, 2 vols. (Cambridge: University Press, 1920), 1:118-123, 130-131, 2:1-11, and F. C. Grant, *The Gospels: Their Origin and Their Growth* (New York: Harper, 1957): 65, 144.

[25] Hunt, *Primitive Gospel Sources*, 184.

[26] Grant, *Gospels, Their Origin and Growth*, 65, 144; cf. Eusebius *Ecclesiastical History* 3.39.1, 14.

prophecies of the Messiah, "a collection of the kind embedded in the Gospel of Matthew."[27]

Yet, this view seems unlikely for significant reasons. First, a similar criticism applies to this view as to the first view above, i.e., in the context of Papias' writings, τα; lovgia most likely refers to both deeds and sayings of Jesus and not to a hypothesized collection of OT proof-texts. This view, therefore, supplies an aberrant meaning to Papias' words. It also makes Grant's assumption regarding τῶν κυριακῶν ... λογίων as referring to OT oracles tenuous since Papias, in the context of Eusebius' discussion, refers to Jesus' sayings and deeds rather than OT sayings, the latter not being in view at all in that context.[28]

Second, the view cannot account for the diversity of text forms in OT quotations in Matthew and for the way he often parallels the LXX rather than the Hebrew OT (e.g., Matt. 1:23; 5:21, 27, 38, 43; 13:14-15; 21:16).[29]

Third, the most likely understanding of the term hJrmhvneusen refers to "translation" of a language, especially in light of his phrase "in the Hebrew language" (Ἐβραΐδι διαλέκτῳ), rather than "interpretation" of OT sayings, the latter being the sense required under this vlew.[30] Furthermore, this Hebrew (i.e., Aramaic) *testimonia* collection may not need to be "translated" especially since the LXX would have been well-established.

---

[27] Grant, *Gospels, Their Origin and Growth*, 65.

[28] Eusebius *Ecclesiastical History* 3.39.1, 14.

[29] Gundry notes, "Of the twenty formal quotations peculiar to Mt, seven are Septuagintal. Seven are non-Septuagintal. In six there is a mixture of Septuagintal and non-Septuagintal" (Robert H. Gundry, *The Use of the Old Testament in St. Matthew's Gospel* [Leiden: E. J. Brill, 1967], 149).

[30] Martin, *New Testament Foundations*, 1:239.

Ta logia *as an error by Papias.* Yet, if some scholars find neither of these two views satisfactory regarding τα; λovγια, then they often envision two alternatives in their discussion of its meaning: either Papias was inaccurate and his testimony should be discounted, or Papias was referring to some other composition of Matthew which is not now extant.

Carson, Moo, and Morris prefer the idea that Papias' statement was partially in error when he asserted a Semitic (i.e. Aramaic) original of Matthew, labeling it as "an intelligent, albeit erroneous, guess."[31] From their point of view Papias spoke from ignorance, especially if he "had no real knowledge of just how much Greek was spoken in first-century Palestine, especially in Galilee."[32] At times, they are ambivalent as to who wrote the gospel bearing Matthew's name, for after discussing the evidence, both pros and cons, for apostolic authorship of the gospel, they conclude "at one level very little hangs on the question of the authorship of this [Matthew's] gospel. By and large, neither its meaning nor its authority are greatly changed if one decides that its author was not an apostle."[33] For them, apostolic, eyewitness origin ultimately carries little weight for the validity of this gospel. Martin holds the same perspective.[34]

Harrison deprecates Papias in a fashion similar to Carson, Moo and Morris, arguing that "Papias, like Jerome, confused the *Gospel according to the Hebrews* or

---

[31] Carson *et al., Introduction to the New Testament,* 70.

[32] Ibid., 71.

[33] Ibid., 74; cf. D. A. Carson, "Matthew," vol. 8 of *Expositor's Bible Commentary.* Frank E. Gaebelein, gen. ed. (Grand Rapids: Zondervan, 1984), 19.

[34] Martin, *New Testament Foundations,* 1:240.

something like it with an Aramaic Matthew."[35] Similarly, Hill comments, "[T]he tradition of Matthean priority rests . . . on a misinterpretation of Papias' statements, or on Papias' misunderstanding of the actual matter to which he was referring."[36]

Significantly, most of these evangelicals who dismiss the testimony of Papias apparently do so because of their acceptance of the historical-critical conclusion that Mark was the first gospel, as expressed in the Two- or Four-Source hypothesis.[37] For them, current (and dogmatic) source-critical conclusions are sufficient to override strong and ancient historical testimony.[38] Yet, in reply, apostolic origin of the gospels is vital for a document that purports to be a record of Jesus' historical ministry on earth. The anonymity of the Matthean gospel argues strongly for the validity of tradition that attached Matthew's name to it because such anonymity is inexplicable apart from its direct association with the apostle Matthew. Matthew was a relatively obscure figure among the Twelve, so no adequate reason exists to explain why the early church would have chosen his name rather than a better-known apostle if he had not indeed written it.

Furthermore, the more reasonable explanation is that Papias, possessing information from highly placed apostolic and eyewitness testimony regarding Matthew, was correct, and that attempts at deprecating Papias border on intellectual presumptuousness. Petrie describes

---

[35] Everett F. Harrison, *Introduction to the New Testament* (Grand Rapids: Eerdmans, 1971), 169.

[36] Hill, *Gospel of Matthew*, 29.

[37] E.g., Carson, Moo and Morris, *Introduction to the New Testament*, 61-85 (esp. 68-69); Martin, *New Testament Foundations*, 1:139-60; 224-43; Hill, *Matthew*, 29-34.

[38] E.g., Carson, "Matthew," 13.

such a casual dismissal of the evidence: "This is the kind of unintentional belittling guess that easily hardens from 'may be' to a firm statement and then becomes a dogmatic basis for further adventures in criticism."[39] Since Papias is not relating his own opinion but citing information derived from firsthand reports of the apostle John and the disciple Ariston, a supposition of Papias' confusion is unlikely. For as Gundry observes, "Possibilities of confusion decrease the closer we approach the time of writing. It is especially hard to think that one of the twelve apostles, John himself, fell into such an error."[40] Interestingly, Papias uses the imperfect tense (e[legen, elegen-"he was saying") to depict how John repeatedly transmitted information to him about Mark's arrangement of topics.[41] Theirs was not just a one-time conversation. Petrie best summarizes Historical Criticism's attack on Papias' credibility well:

> This testimony is on much firmer ground than the best speculative guesses of the twentieth century, and it must be fairly and fully reckoned with in the quest for Gospel backgrounds. Failing substantial evidence to contradict it or to turn its meaning, it is not to be dismissed because of its inconvenience for current hypotheses. If it does not accord with these hypotheses, it is the hypotheses that must be considered anew. For the one is tangible evidence from a competent, informed, and credible witness; the rest, however attractive or even dazzling they appear, lack its substantiality.[42]

---

[39] Petrie, "Authorship of 'The Gospel According to Matthew,'" 29.

[40] Gundry, *Matthew, A Commentary*, 618.

[41] Eusebius *Ecclesiastical History* 3.39.15.

[42] Petrie, "The Authorship of Matthew," 32. Strangely, Hagner, a Markan prioritist, agrees: "[I]t seems better to take this early piece of evidence seriously rather than to dismiss it as being dead wrong. Papias

Ta logia as a canonical Greek Matthew.

A fourth view of Papias' meaning takes τα; lovgia to refer to the canonical Greek version of Matthew's gospel and exonerates Papias as an accurate reporter, but says his readers misunderstood him. Reflecting a concept similar to Kürzinger,[43] Gundry asserts that rather than a linguistic sense Papias' expression "in the Hebrew dialect" (Ἑβραΐδι διαλέκτῳ) has a literary sense, referring to a Semitic style: "In describing Matthew, then, 'a Hebrew dialect' means a Hebrew way of presenting Jesus' messiahship."[44] With this approach, the verb ἡρμήνευσεν had the sense of "explain" rather than "translate."

Moreover, Kürzinger points out that immediately before Papias' statement regarding Matthew, he describes Mark's composition of his gospel as reflecting Peter's testimony. There Papias calls Mark the "interpreter" (ἡρμήνευτες;", hermeneutes [—Eusebius *Ecclesiastical History* 3.39.15]) of Peter. Kürzinger insists that this cannot mean that Mark was Peter's "translator," but must have been the "interpreter" of that preached or spoken by Peter.[45] Thus, Papias' statement regarding Matthew must mean that everyone "passed on" or "interpreted" Matthew's Greek gospel to the world as he was able.

---

had reason for saying what he did . . . we do well to attempt to make sense of his testimony" (Donald A. Hanger, *Matthew 1-13*, vol. 33A of *Word Biblical Commentary*, David A. Hubbard and Glenn W. Barker, eds. (Waco, Tx.: Word, 1993), xlvi.

[43] Josef Kürzinger, "Das Papiaszeugnis und die Erstgestalt des Matthäusevangeliums," *Biblische Zeitschrift* 4 (1960): 19-38; cf. *idem*, "Irenäus und sein Zeugnis zur Sprache des Matthäusevangeliums," *New Testament Studies* 10 (1963), 108-15.

[44] Gundry, *Matthew: A Commentary*, 619-20.

[45] Cf. Kürzinger, "Das Papiaszeugnis," 22-23, 27-30.

A first response to that analysis notes that although the sense of argumentational style is a possible meaning of διαλέκτῳ /,[46] it is a more remote and secondary sense. The most natural understanding of διαλέκτος (dialektos) is "language," not "interpretation."[47] Also, the term in combination with the noun JEbrai?di (*Hebraidi*, lit. "Hebrew" but most likely a reference the Aramaic language) and the verb eJrmhneuvein (*hermeneuein*, "to interpret") points to the latter's natural meaning of "translate (a language)" rather than to an alleged Semitic style.

Second, the church fathers understood Papias' statement as referring to language. Without exception they held that the apostle Matthew wrote the canonical Matthew and that he wrote it first in a Semitic language.[48]

Third, all six occurrences of the word διαλέκτος in the NT refer to human languages rather than to a particular style of argument (Acts 1:19; 2:6, 8; 21:40; 22:2; 26:14).[49]

---

[46] E.g., cf. Liddell and Scott, *A Greek English Lexicon*, rev. and augmented by Henry Stuart Jones, with a 1968 Supplement (Oxford: At the Clarendon, 1940), 401.

[47] E.g., *BAGD*, 185; James P. Louw and Eugene A. Nida, *Clarendon Press of the New Testament Based on Semantic Domains* (New York: United Bible Societies, 1988), 1:389 (33.1).

[48] E.g., Irenaeus *Against Heresies* 3.1.1 (quoted in Eusebius *Ecclesiastical History* 5.8.2); Tertullian (*Against Marcion* 4.2); Pantaenus, cited by Eusebius (*Ecclesiastical History* 5.10.3); Origen (quoted by Eusebius in *Ecclesiastical History* 6.25.3-6); Eusebius himself (*Ecclesiastical History* 3.24.5-6); and Jerome *Preface to the Commentary on Saint Matthew*; *Lives of Illustrious Men* 2.3.

[49] Gundry argues that these NT occurrences of diavlekto" (*dialektos*, "language" or "dialect") are articular (and thus definite) so that human language is clearly in mind in these passages. In contrast, Papias's reference does not have the article (i.e. JEbrai?di dialevktw/, Hebraidi dialektōi, "Hebrew dialect"). He concludes that Papias's reference should be considered indefinite ("a Hebrew way of presenting Jesus' messiahship" or Semitic style of argument) rather than definite ("the Semitic language").

These arguments render the view of Kürzinger and Gundry as very improbable.

A significant observation notes that the common thread of all four viewpoints of Papias' words discussed so far is an *a priori* assumption of validity of the Two-Document Hypothesis. As a result, they all attempt to find a way either to diminish the force of Papias' words, dismiss his information as inaccurate or wrong, or superimpose a totally foreign understanding. Survival of the cherished synoptic hypothesis drives them to pursue such tactics as Gundry illustrates in his discussion of Papias' words: "[I]t is the currently prevalent and well-substantiated opinion that our Greek Matthew shows many signs of drawing in large part on the Gospel of Mark, also written in Greek."[50]

Gundry goes one step further in his analysis of Papias' words. He takes them to indicate that Matthew deliberately corrected Mark. Immediately before Papias' comments about Matthew (Eusebius *Ecclesiastical History* 3.39.16), Eusebius quotes Papias' description of the composition of Mark:

> "And the Presbyter [John] used to say this, 'Mark became Peter's interpreter and wrote accurately all that he remembered, not, indeed, in order, of the things said or done by the Lord. For he had not heard the Lord, nor had he followed him, but later on, as I said, followed Peter, who used to give teaching as necessity demanded but not making, as it were, an arrangement of the Lord's oracles, so that Mark

---

See Gundry, *Matthew*, 629-20. Yet, in reply, the article is not necessary for Papias to mean "language." The force of JEbrai?di ("Hebrew") with dialevktw/ is sufficient to make the term definite without the article. For instances where the article is not necessary to make a noun definite, consult Daniel B. Wallace, *Greek Grammar Beyond the Basics* (Grand Rapids: Zondervan, 1996), 245-54.

[50] Gundry, *Matthew: A Commentary*, 618.

did nothing in wrong in writing down single points as he remembered them. For to one thing he gave attention, to leave out nothing of what he had heard and to make no false statements in them.'" This is related by Papias about Mark.⁵¹

Since the statements come before Papias' comments about Matthew's gospel, Gundry contends that they prove that Mark wrote before Matthew. In a nutshell, he argues that the sequence and nature of discussion in this section indicate that Matthew should be understood as a deliberate corrective to Mark. He notes that Papias' statements that Mark's gospel was written "not, indeed, in order" and "not making . . . an arrangement of the Lord's oracles" comes immediately before Papias' discussion of Matthew and how he "collected" (συνετάξατο, sunetavxato) his oracles. Gundry contends, Matthew did it "for the precise purpose of bringing order out of the chaos in Mark."⁵²

However, a few observations show Gundry's contentions to be tenuous. First, Eusebius is quoting *detached* statements of Papias regarding Mark and Matthew so that the sequence of the gospels means nothing nor does any alleged dependence among the gospels surface in the order of discussion in the text.⁵³

---

⁵¹ Eusebius *Ecclesiastical History* 3.39.15.

⁵² Gundry, *Matthew: A Commentary*, 614.

⁵³ Gundry contends that the ou\∍n in Ecclesiastical History 3.39.16 refers back "to the statement about Mark" and therefore ties the thought about Mark and Matthew together. As a result," ou\∍n contains an immmensely important implication for synoptic studies . . . Matthew's reason for writing is in view . . . Matthew wrote his gospel for the precise purpose of bringing order out of the chaos in Mark." Gundry, *Matthew: A Commentary*, 614. However, contrary to Gundry, his contention of a link through ou\∍n is dubious. The ou\∍n grammatically draws an inferential conclusion to the discussion about Mark, going back by 3.39.14. Furthermore, peri; de; occurs after the ou\∍n and functions to

Second, such a theory indicates the absolute paucity of evidence for the Two-Document Hypothesis in ancient tradition. Its proponents must attempt to make something out of nothing in a desperate attempt at proving their *a priori* and *dogmatic* assumption that colors everything they analyze.

Papias' words (and Eusebius' citation and discussion) do not constitute any type of proof for Markan priority or literary dependence between Matthew and Mark. They add absolutely nothing to an understanding of any relationship between Matthew or Mark (or the other gospels for that matter). Eusebius' disjointed citation of Papias' words about Mark coming before that same historian's citation of Papias' words about Matthew's gospel have no relevance to that issue. Such alleged evidence goes far beyond what the statements indicate and is blatantly *non sequitur*. As a matter of fact, Papias' statements here actually constitute evidence against an assumed literary dependence, for he remarked that Mark depended on Peter for the contents of his gospel!

Ta logia as an early edition of Matthew's gospel.

A final view, distinct from the others (and also from their synoptic hypotheses) is that Papias referred to an earlier edition of Matthew written entirely in Hebrew (i.e., Aramaic) that Matthew wrote first. That was perhaps a proto-Matthew, i.e., a shorter version that eventually came to be incorporated into (not necessarily translated from but contained within) an expanded Greek version,

---

introduce a new, unrelated information concerning Matthew's gospel (cf. Paul's introduction of new subject matter in 1 Cor. 7:1, 25; 8:1; 12:1; 16:1, 12), thus demonstrating that these two thoughts of Papias about Mark and Matthew most likely are not linked together nor in any way indicative of Gundry's contention for Matthew as a corrective of Mark.

i.e., the canonical Gospel of Matthew.⁵⁴ Thus, Papias indicated that Matthew wrote first (prior to the other gospels) and that in so doing, he produced an initial Aramaic edition. The Aramaic edition served as a model and/or source for some of the contents of his Greek edition that he most likely produced as a fresh work soon after he wrote the Aramaic one.⁵⁵

Several arguments support this proposal. First, it permits Papias to speak for himself and allows for an understanding of his words in their natural sense. Since he was closest to the events and relied on excellent sources, his information must have priority over speculative modern hypotheses.

Second, an expanded Greek version would have been quickly helpful among Matthew's targeted Jewish audience, especially those hellenized Jews who no longer spoke Hebrew (the *Diaspora* [Acts 6:1]). Although Matthew concentrated his efforts at first among Hebraistic Jews who spoke Aramaic, such a gospel would have

---

⁵⁴ The canonical Greek Version shows no signs of being translated from Aramaic. For example, in certain places it transliterates Aramaic into Greek before giving a Greek translation—e.g., Matt. 1:23, ΔEmmanouh/l, o¢ e˙stin meqermhneuo/menon meqΔ hJmwΘn oJ qeo/ß

(*Emmanouēl, ho estin methermēneuomenon meth' hēmōn ho theos*— "Immanuel, which is interpreted 'God with us'"); Matt. 27:33, Golgoqa0, o¢ e˙stin Krani÷ou To/poß lego/menoß *(Golgotha, ho estin Kraniou Topos legomenos*, "Golgotha, which is called 'the Place of the Skull'"); cf. also Matt. 27:46. Also, the Greek Matthew provides explanations of local customs among the Jews that would have been unnecessary for an Aramaic-speaking audience (e.g., Matt. 27:15). Though the Greek Matthew is not a translation, Matthew may have produced an expanded version of the life of Christ that incorporated much of the original Aramaic without being a direct translation of it. Such an entirely reworked version would have suited the needs of the Diaspora Jews and others.

⁵⁵ Louis Berkhof, *New Testament Introduction* (Grand Rapids: Eerdman-Sevensma, 1915), 64-71; Henry Clarence Thiessen, *Introduction to the New Testament* (Grand Rapids: Eerdmans, 1943), 137.

limited appeal outside of the land of the Jews. Tradition has it that Matthew eventually left the environs of Jerusalem to minister among non-Aramaic-speaking peoples.[56] The dominance of Greek in the Hellenistic world would have impelled him to produce another edition. Because he was a former tax-collector for the Romans, he would most likely have been conversant in Greek as well as Aramaic,[57] thus facilitating the writing of both versions. Once the Greek Matthew became current in the church, the limited appeal of Aramaic caused that edition to fall into disuse. Papias' statement that "each interpreted" Matthew's gospel [Aramaic version] "as best he could" probably hints at the reason why Matthew would have quickly produced a Greek version: to facilitate the understanding of his gospel in the universal language of Greek.

Third, this view accords with the very early and consistent manuscript ascription of the Gospel to Matthew (KATA MAQQAION, *KATA MATHTHAION*, "According to Matthew").[58] The title is not a part of the original text, but no positive evidence exists that the book ever circulated without this title. Moreover, the ascription has a very early date, approximately A.D. 125.[59] As Guthrie

---

[56] Eusebius *Ecclesiastical History* 3.24.5-6; Hippolytus *On the Twelve Apostles* 7; cf. D. A. Hagner, "Matthew," in vol. 3 of *ISBE*, Geoffrey W. Bromiley, gen. ed. (Grand Rapids: Eerdmans, 1986), 280.

[57] Matt. 9:9-14; Mark 2:13-17; Luke 5:27-32; cf. Gundry, *Use of the Old Testament*, 183; Edgar J. Goodspeed, *Matthew, Apostle and Evangelist* (Philadelphia: John C. Winston, 1959), 42-47.

[58] Davies and Allison try to explain away the title in light of their assumption of that Mark wrote first and the Matthean gospel could not have been written by an apostle. Their case lacks persuasiveness in light of consistent manuscript evidence, however (cf. W. D. Davies and Dale C. Allison, *The Gospel According to Matthew*, International Critical Commentary [Edinburgh: T & T Clark, 1988], 1:58).

[59] Ropes reasons, "Probably as early in the second century as the year 125, someone, in some place, or some group of persons, assembled

notes, "the title cannot be dismissed too lightly, for it has the support of ancient tradition and this must be the starting point of the discussion regarding authorship."[60] Very early and consistent ascription of the Greek gospel to Matthew would indicate that the transfer of connection from Matthew's Aramaic version mentioned by Papias to the Greek gospel occurred at a very early stage well into the first century. Such a very early stage would have placed Greek Matthew into a period when people, such as surviving apostles, eyewitnesses and other who possessed first-hand knowledge regarding the Gospel would have linked the Aramaic and Greek versions together as coming from the hand of Matthew. Moreover, during this strategic early period the prevention of such linkage could also have occurred if such attempts at linkage were inaccurate.

This early ascription coordinates well with the very early and widespread influence of Greek Matthew in the early church in the period before Irenaeus. Significant Matthean influence can be seen in such early second century works as 1 Clement (ca. A.D. 81-96), Barnabas (ca. A.D. 70-135), the Letters of Ignatius of Antioch (ca. A.D. 98-117), 2 Clement (ca. A.D. 138-142), Polycarp (*to the Philippians* ca. A.D. 98-117; d. ca. 156 or 167), Aristedes of Athens (fl. A.D. 123), Justin Martyr (d. ca. 165), Tatian (fl. ca. A.D. 160-170) and the Didache (ca. A.D. late first century to mid-second century), to mention only a few.[61]

---

for the use and convenience of the churches the only four Greek books describing the life and teachings of Jesus Christ which were then believed to be of great antiquity and worthy of a place in such a collection" (J. H. Ropes, *The Synoptic Gospels*, 2nd Impression with New Preface [Cambridge, Ma.: Harvard University, 1960], 103).

[60] Donald Guthrie, *New Testament Introduction*, 2nd Edition (Downers Grove, Ill.: InterVarsity, 1990), 156-57.

[61] The reader is once again directed to Massaux's excellent cataloguing of Matthew's extensive influence in Christian literature during this early period (consult Massaux, *The Influence of the Gospel of Saint*

Such influence finds its most reasonable explanation in Matthean authorship of the Greek Gospel as well as the Aramaic version discussed by Papias. Furthermore, this unbroken stream of tradition indicates that Matthew was responsible for both versions of the Gospel that bears his name. While the Aramaic version was helpful for Matthew's work among Jews, his departure to work with gentiles resulted in his issuance of the Greek version in the lingua franca of the day in order to facilitate the spread the good news regarding Messiah among gentiles.

Fourth, though patristic witnesses like Papias uniformly spoke of an Aramaic original for the gospel, they accepted the Greek Matthew as unquestionably authoritative and coming from the apostle Matthew himself.[62] They offered no explanation concerning the change in language.[63] Most likely, that indicates their regard for the Greek Matthew as authoritative and substantially representative of the Hebrew ta logia.[64] Besides, all references to the Gospel of Matthew in the early church fathers reflect the Greek Matthew rather than the Hebrew. They never viewed the Greek Gospel of Matthew as inferior but as equal or better than the other Greek canonical gospels in terms of its authority and influence.

The Matthean authorship of both the Greek and Aramaic versions is strengthened by the unlikelihood of

---

Matthew, Books 1-3. For the composition dates of some of these works, consult Robert M. Grant, gen. ed. *The Apostolic Fathers. A New Translation and Commentary* (New York: Thomas Nelson & Sons, 1964): 1:38, 46-48, 64, 71; 3:42-43, 76-77; 5:4.

[62] See note 48 for a list of fathers who supported this.

[63] Jerome who wrote, "who afterwards translated it into Greek is not certainly known," is a possible exception (Jerome *Lives of Illustrious Men* 2.3).

[64] Hiebert, *Introduction to the New Testament*, 1:53.

such a transfer occurring between documents that differed significantly in language and in content unless Matthew himself did produce both versions. The traditions of Matthean authorship for both versions are so significantly early and consistent that authorship by Matthew himself constitutes the most reasonable explanation for both streams of tradition.

Fifth, the universal ascription of the Greek Matthew to the apostle Matthew and the failure of tradition to mention any other possible author except Matthew renders unconvincing any suggestion that the early church forgot the true author of the work. Only a brief span of 50 to 60 years passed between its composition and the statements of Papias. A less-prominent apostle such as Matthew would not have been a likely candidate to receive credit for such an important and influential document as the Greek Matthew unless he did indeed write it. As indicated earlier in this chapter, "of all the New Testament Writings, the Gospel of Mt. was the one whose literary influence was the most widespread and the most profound in Christian literature that extended into the last decades of the second century. . . . [T]he first gospel remained the gospel par excellence. . . . The gospel was, therefore, the normative fact of Christian life. It created the background for ordinary Christianity."[65]

The only adequate explanation for the gospel's influence and overwhelming popularity in the early church is its apostolic authorship. That one of the Twelve wrote it soon after writing his Aramaic ta logia and before Mark and Luke wrote their gospels is far and away the most satisfactory explanation for the facts that remain from early church history.

In light of the evidence, unless someone feels compelled to embrace historical-critical scholarship's *a*

---

[65] Massaux, *Influence of the Gospel of Saint Matthew*, 3:186-187.

priori assumption of Markan priority, the testimony of Papias is credible and supportive of Matthean priority and Matthean authorship of the gospel that bears Matthew's name.

IRENAEUS

Irenaeus (b. ca. A.D. 115-120 and martyred ca. A.D. 200), an immigrant from Asia Minor, was presbyter of the church at Lyons in Gaul. He was one of the early church's most able apologists and theologians, writing against Marcion and the Gnostics with His work *Refutation and Overthrow of Knowledge Falsely So-called* which tradition has more conveniently labeled *Against Heresies* (completed ca. A.D. 185).[66]

In his youth he claims to have been a disciple of Polycarp (b. ca. A.D. 70 and d. ca. A.D. 155-160). He writes, "Polycarp . . . was not only instructed by apostles and conversed with many who had seen the Lord, but was also appointed bishop by apostles in Asia in the church in Smyrna."[67] Irenaeus continues, "We also saw him [i.e., Polycarp] in our childhood. . . . He [i.e., Polycarp] constantly taught those things which he had learnt from the apostles, which also are the tradition of the church, which alone are true."[68] As reported by Eusebius, Polycarp, in turn, was a disciple of the Apostle John:

> "I [i.e. Irenaeus] remember the events of those days more clearly than those which happened recently, for what we learn as children

---

[66] Eusebius *Ecclesiastical History* 5.7.1. Two major writings of Irenaeus have survived. In addition to *Against Heresies*, he also wrote *Demonstration of the Apostolic Preaching*, the latter being an instructional book demonstrating that the Christian faith fulfills the OT, first published in the twentieth century.

[67] Eusebius *Ecclesiastical History* 4.14.3.

[68] Ibid., 4.14.3-4; 5.20.5-6; cf. Irenaeus *Against Heresies* 3.3.4.

grows up with the soul and is united to it, so that I can speak even of the place in which the blessed Polycarp sat and disputed, how he came in and went out, the character of his life, the discourses which he made to the people, how he [Polycarp] reported his intercourse with John and with the others who had seen the Lord, how he remembered their words, and what were the things concerning the Lord which he had heard from them . . . and how Polycarp had received them from the eyewitnesses of the word of life."[69]

Besides Polycarp, Irenaeus also had met and conversed with many apostolic and sub-apostolic fathers of Asia Minor and obtained information from them about the life and teachings of the Lord and the activities of the early church.[70] He thus reflected information from many sources and not only from his own childhood memories. He also had traveled extensively (e.g., from Asia Minor to Gaul and also the church in Rome), so that his information is not from an isolated region but widespread.

Irenaeus writes the following regarding the gospels:

Now Matthew published among the Hebrews a written gospel also in their own tongue, while Peter and Paul were preaching in Rome and founding the church. But after their death, Mark also, the disciple and interpreter of Peter, himself handed down to us in writing the things which were preached by Peter, and Luke also, who was a follower of Paul, put down in a book the gospel which was preached by him. Then John, the disciple of the Lord, who had

---

[69] Eusebius *Ecclesiastical History* 5.20.5-6

[70] Irenaeus *Against Heresies* 2.22.5; 4.27.1; 4.32.1; 5.36.2.

even rested on his breast, himself also gave forth the gospel, while he was living in Ephesus in Asia."[71]

Proponents of the Two-Document Hypothesis dismiss Irenaeus' assertion as useless because they assert, he was merely repeating Papias. Filson argues, "But note this: Papias is the key witness. Irenaeus, for example, obviously knows and uses Papias as an authority. No tradition demonstrably independent of Papias exists."[72] Nineham does the same: "The testimony of early Christian writers subsequent to Papias, such as Irenaeus, Clement of Alexandria, Origen, and Jerome, need not be discussed at length, for it is not clear that these writers had any trustworthy source of information other than the Papias tradition."[73] Streeter, the great advocate of the Four-Document Hypothesis, deprecates Irenaeus' ability to testify regarding Polycarp's connection to John, dismissing the evidence because of Irenaeus' youth. He says he was too young to tell to which "John" Polycarp referred.[74]

Petrie drives to the heart of their problem, noting, "There is in the document [i.e., the writings of Irenaeus] no hint of dependence [i.e., on Papias]. Indeed, Irenaeus was sufficiently close to the authorities of Papias to have gathered this information on his own."[75] In addition,

---

[71] Ibid., 3.1.1-4; cited also in Eusebius's *Ecclesiastical History* 5.8.1-4.

[72] Floyd Filson, *A Commentary on the Gospel According to Matthew*, 2nd ed. (London: Adam & Charles Black, 1971), 16.

[73] D. E. Nineham, *St. Mark* (Philadelphia: Westminster,1963), 39 n.

[74] Streeter apparently held that the Apostle John and the Elder John to whom Papias referred were two different individuals (Streeter, *Four Gospels*, 444).

[75] Petrie, "Authorship of 'The Gospel According to Matthew,'" 29.

Irenaeus was more than likely at least 15 years old, old enough "to understand the meaning of Polycarp's words and also to distinguish between the Apostle John and any other John."[76] As Lightfoot reasoned, "A pupil of Polycarp, at all events, was not likely to be misinformed here."[77] Besides nullifying the Two- or Four-Source Theory's view of Markan priority, Irenaeus' testimony also negates literary dependence of Mark on Matthew as proposed by the Two-Gospel Hypothesis, because it states that Mark depended on Peter's preaching, not on the other written gospels of Matthew or Luke, for his information.

In sum, proponents of Two-Document Hypothesis must either reject, ignore, or explain away much of the evidence by any means possible, because acceptance of its credibility would reinforce the fact of Matthew's gospel being written prior to the other gospels. That constitutes a strong testimony either against their assumption of the priority of Mark or, for that matter, against the idea that Mark depended on Matthew instead of Peter's preaching as held by the Two-Gospel Hypothesis. The belittling of Irenaeus by advocates of the Two-Document Hypothesis notwithstanding, Irenaeus' testimony is credible and important in its own right, constituting an independent and reliable witness for information regarding Matthew as the first gospel.

Worthy of observation also in this section is Irenaeus' failure to make a substantial distinction between the Aramaic and Greek versions as coming from Matthew.[78] For example, in *Against Heresies* 3.1.1 Irenaeus discusses all four gospels. In this discussion, he mentions only the

---

[76] A. C. Perumalil, "Are not Papias and Irenaeus competent to report on the Gospels?," *Expository Times* 91 (August 1980): 336.

[77] J. B. Lightfoot, *Supernatural Religion*, 142.

[78] Irenaeus *Against Heresies* 3.1.1; also cited by Eusebius *Ecclesiastical History* 5.8.2.

Hebrew Matthew. Yet, in the work he shows a close familiar with Greek Matthew by referring to it frequently.[79] That indicates that he equated the Aramaic Matthew with the Greek Matthew and intimately connected them with each other.

Although the statement cited follows the order Matthew, Mark, Luke and John, the sequence in this passage is unique to Irenaeus.[80] He generally follows the order of Matthew, Luke, Mark and John at other places which, as Campenhausen notes, "would seem therefore to be the order most familiar to Irenaeus himself."[81] Yet, in another place, he follows the sequence John-Luke-Matthew-Mark (*Against Heresies* 3.2.8) perhaps because of theological rather than historical, reasons.[82] Since Irenaeus follows a variety of sequences when mentioning the gospels, he is not of much help in establishing a sequence of composition, but he does offer support for the priority of Matthew as first to be composed and apparent support for the composition of Luke before Mark.

---

[79] To cite only a few random examples, cp. Irenaeus *Against Heresies* "Preface" 2 with Matt. 10:26; cp. 1.1.3 with Matt. 20:1-16; cp. 1.3.5 with Matt.10:21, 34; cp. 1.6.1 with Matt. 5:13-14; cp. 1.8. with Matt. 26:38-39; 27:46; cp. 3.8.1 with Matt. 6:24.

[80] Irenaeus in this context appears to be setting forth an apologetic regarding the content of each gospel as being inspired by the Holy Spirit and united in testimony about the true contents of the gospel in contrast to the teaching of heretics. He is not necessarily setting forth a strict compositional order (cf. *Against Heresies* 3.2.1).

[81] Hans von Campenhausen, *The Formation of the Christian Bible* (Philadelphia: Fortress, 1972), 195 n. 243; cf. e.g., Irenaeus *Against Heresies* 3.9.1-11.8; 4.6.1.

[82] Campenhausen explains this order of John-Luke-Matthew-Mark as corresponding "to the various epochs of salvation history" from Irenaeus's perspective (Campenhausen, *Formation of the Christian Bible*, 195 n. 243.

CLEMENT OF ALEXANDRIA

The origins of Christianity in Alexandria are obscure. The movement must have appeared there at a relatively early date since it appears firmly established at least as early as ca. late second century.[83] According to Eusebius, Pantaenus was the earliest leader of the catechetical school in Alexandria ca. A.D. 185. He as a converted Stoic philosopher whom Eusebius describes as "especially eminent."[84] Eventually, Pantaenus was "appointed as a herald for the gospel of Christ to the heathen in the East, and was sent as far as India."[85] Upon arrival, Pantaenus allegedly discovered that the Hebrew version of Matthew's gospel had preceded him there, being left by the Apostle Bartholomew.[86] That tradition corroborates information from both Papias and Irenaeus about Matthew writing originally in Hebrew (or Aramaic).

Clement of Alexandria (ca. A.D. 150-215) located in Alexandria and became a pupil of Pantaenus.[87] In time, he distinguished himself as a scholar and became a teacher for over twenty years in Alexandria, succeeding Pantaenus as the leader of the school. At the outbreak of persecution under Severus in A.D. 202, he left Alexandria, never to return. In spite of periods of intense persecution, the school gained great prominence and importance. Beyond that, few facts regarding Clement are available. Nothing certain is known concerning his parentage or early

---

[83] Williston Walker and Richard A. Norris, David W. Lotz and Robert T. Handy, *A History of the Christian Church*, 4th ed. (New York: Charles Scribner's Sons, 1985), 87.

[84] Eusebius *Ecclesiastical History* 5.10.1-2.

[85] Ibid., 5.10.2.

[86] Ibid., 5.10.2-3.

[87] Ibid., 5.11.1-2.

training.[88] Most likely, he was not a Christian during his early years. According to Eusebius, however, he was "the namesake of the pupil of the apostles who had once ruled the church of Rome"[89] while his name reflects his connection with the Egyptian city of Alexandria where he accomplished all his important works. His extant works are *Exhortation to the Greeks, Pedagogue, Stromateis* or *Miscellanies, Who is the rich man that shall be saved?* and some fragments from *Selections from the Prophets* which is a brief commentary on portions of the Scripture.

Information from Clement is of basic importance in determining the order of composition of the gospels, for not only was he a preeminent early church scholar as head of the Alexandrian school but was also in personal contact with a number of church elders from different parts of the Mediterranean world and their information regarding that order. The following quotation of Clement by Eusebius reveals Clement's widespread network of information:

> This work [i.e. *Stromateis*] is not a writing composed for show, but notes stored up for my old age, a remedy against forgetfulness, an image without art, and a sketch of those clear and vital words which I was privileged to hear, and of blessed and truly notable men. Of these one, the Ionian, was in Greece, another in South Italy, a third in Coele-Syria, another in Egypt, and there were others in the East, one of them an Assyrian, another in Palestine of Hebrew origin. But when I had met the last, and in

---

[88] Butterworth says he may have been an Athenian by birth (G. W. Butterworth, "Introduction," *Clement of Alexandria*, trans. by G. W. Butterworth, The Loeb Classical Library [London: William Heinemann, 1919], xi).

[89] Eusebius, *Ecclesiastical History* 5.11.1

power he was indeed the first, I hunted him out from his concealment in Egypt and found rest.[90]

The last elder in Egypt referred to is most likely Pantaenus. Since he probably met Pantaenus in the latter part of the second century, the testimony that the various elders passed on would reflect well back into the first half of that century.[91]

What is important for the present study is that Clement's widespread information furnishes important additional information about the order of the synoptics. Eusebius quotes him as follows regarding this order:

> And again in the same books Clement has inserted a tradition of the primitive elders with regard to the order of the Gospels, as follows. He said that those Gospels were first written which include the genealogies, but that the Gospel according to Mark came into being in this manner: When Peter had publicly preached the word at Rome, and by the Spirit had proclaimed the Gospel, that those present, who were many, exhorted Mark, as one who had followed him for a long time and remembered what had been spoken, to make a record of what was said; and that he did this, and distributed the Gospel among those that asked him. And that when the matter came to Peter's knowledge he neither strongly forbade it nor urged it forward. But that John, last of all, conscious that the outward facts had been set

---

[90] Ibid., 5.11.3-4; Clement *Stromateis* 1.1.1.11; cf. also J. Stevenson, *The New Eusebius*, rev. by W. H. C. Frend (London: SPCK, 1987), 180 [*Stromateis* 1.1.11.1-3; *Ecclesiastical History* 5.11.3-5].

[91] William R. Farmer, "The Patristic Evidence Reexamined: A Response to George Kennedy," in *New Synoptic Studies*, William R. Farmer, ed. (Macon, Ga.: Mercer University, 1983), 7.

forth in the Gospels, was urged on by his disciples, and, divinely moved by the Spirit, composed a spiritual Gospel. This is Clement's account.[92]

Several important features emerge from those words. First, Clement supplies *unique* information when revealing that the gospels with genealogies (Matthew and Luke) originated before Mark. A scholar of his stature was not likely merely to repeat information without careful investigation. Though Clement does not reveal whether Matthew was first and Luke second or Matthew second and Luke first, he does clearly indicate Mark's third position after Matthew and Luke and not before them as modern historical-critical theories such as Two- and Four-Document Hypotheses maintain.

Moreover, the information from Clement does not contradict Matthew's being first but is an important supplement to information gleaned from other church fathers (e.g., Papias, Irenaeus, Tertullian). The others make plain that Matthew was first, thereby placing Luke second in sequence when combined with Clement's information. Like Irenaeus, Clement places the apostle John's gospel last, saying John wrote it with full awareness of the other three and designed it to supplement the "synoptic" accounts as a "spiritual Gospel." The order of composition, then, was Matthew first, Luke second, Mark third, and John last.

Third, very important in evaluating Clement's information in regard to any proposed solution to the Synoptic Problem is that the tradition he passed on did not come just from a single elder in a single locality but from "a tradition of the primitive elders" (paravdosin tw'n

---

[92] Eusebius *Ecclesiastical History* 6.14.5-7; Clement *Hypotyposeis* 6. The quotation comes from Eusebius, *The Ecclesiastical History, Volume II*, trans. by J. E. L. Oulton, The Loeb Classical Library (Cambridge, Ma.: Harvard University Press, 1932), 46-59.

ajnevkaqen presbutevrwn, *paradosin tøn anekathen presbuterøn*) scattered widely throughout the Christian community. That indicates that it was a tradition known and received in different places some time in the early to mid-second century. Clement's wide travels made this information all the more significant, because it represents a strong tradition in the early church, not merely a fanciful whim of Clement and a few others. As a result, one cannot easily dismiss such information.

Fourth, according to Eusebius in *Ecclesiastical History* 2.16.1, Mark helped found the church at Alexandria and was its first overseer. For Clement to place Mark's gospel third in order of composition is, therefore, all the more important. Gamba notes, "He [Clement] would have no reason at all to place Mark's gospel after the other two that contain a genealogy of Jesus, unless it was for a definite and grounded persuasion of historical nature."[93] That reinforces the strength and reliability of Clement's testimony.

TERTULLIAN

Tertullian (ca. A.D. 160-ca. 225), an exact contemporary of Clement of Alexandria, constitutes a prime witness to the faith of the African church regarding the authenticity of the gospels. Despite his eventual Montanist proclivities, he was the outstanding apologist of the Western church of his time.[94]

---

[93] Giuseppe Fiov. Gamba, "A Further Reexamination of Evidence from Early Tradition," in *New Synoptic Studies*, William R. Farmer, ed. (Macon, Ga.: Mercer University, 1983), 21 n. 10. For further discussion of other ancient documents that suppor Clement's tradition, see ibid., 21-29.

[94] Tertullian became a Montanist in the very early part of the third century A.D. (cf. Earle E. Cairns, *Christianity Though the Centuries* [Grand Rapids: Zondervan, 1996], 106-7].

Little is known of his life except that he was a native of Carthage whose father had been a Roman centurion on duty in that city. He knew and used both Latin and Greek and loved the classics. He became a proficient lawyer and taught public speaking and law in Rome, where he became a convert to Christianity. His goal was the development of a sound Western theology and the defeat of all false philosophical and pagan forces opposed to Christianity.[95]

Tertullian's importance for gospel study lies especially in the fact that he witnessed to the tradition of all Western Christianity, especially the tradition of Rome. His treatise, *Against Marcion* (ca. A.D. 207-212), is especially relevant to the composition of the gospels, because he affirms that apostles wrote Matthew and John, that Mark's gospel reflects Peter's preaching, and that Paul was the sponsor of Luke.

Regarding the four gospels, Tertullian reported that "the evangelical Testament has Apostles as its authors."[96] Here Tertullian makes no distinction between an Aramaic and Hebrew Matthew but considers the Greek Matthew has come from the apostle Matthew himself. Since Tertullian was a lawyer and orator by profession and an outstanding apologist against the heretic Marcion in his *Treatise Against Marcion* where he mentions the gospels' composition, he most probably had his information correct concerning the traditions behind the four gospels. He saw no grounds at all for setting aside this tradition as he attacked Marcion's stance. Any possibility of the facts being wrong would have weakened his attack against Marcion. That his comments corroborate as well as supplement the traditions of Papias, Irenaeus, and Clement strengthens his case even more.

---

[95] Cairns, *Christianity Through the Centuries*, p. 106.

[96] Tertullian *Against Marcion* 4.5.3; cf. ibid., 4.2.1-5.

ORIGEN

Origen (ca. A.D. 185-253) was born into a Christian family in Alexandria. At the age of eighteen, because of his renowned scholarship, he became Clement of Alexandria's successor as the principal Christian teacher in that city after Clement left due to the persecution under Septimus Severus in A.D. 202.[97] Although an eclectic Middle Platonism that was prevalent in Alexandria and in the East adversely affected his thought and gave him a strong propensity toward an allegorical hermeneutic, he was the most remarkable scholar of his time in depth and breadth of learning.

Origen's extant works evidence his profound scholarship. Unfortunately, most of his writings have perished, but he may have written over six thousand works. Several salient examples of his scholarship are representative of the rest. His *Hexapla*, in which several Hebrew and Greek versions of the OT are arranged in parallel columns, constitutes the beginnings of textual criticism. One of his greatest contributions was his work *De Principiis* (ca. A.D. 230), which exists only in a Latin version by Rufinus. It is the first Christian treatise of systematic theology. In the fourth book of that work, he set forth his allegorical method of interpretation. In *Against Celsus* he devised an apologetic defense against the anti-Christian Platonist Celsus. Yet, the majority of his writings took the form of an exegetical commentary on Scripture.

Origen was also widely traveled, having visited Rome (ca. A.D. 211-212), where he met Hippolytus, and Arabia (ca. A.D. 213-214). In ca. A.D. 215 when emperor Caracalla drove all teachers of philosophy from Alexandria, Origen traveled to Caesarea in Palestine. He resumed his teaching in Alexandria ca. A.D. 216 and

---

[97] Cf. Eusebius *Ecclesiastical History* 6.1-8, 16, 29, 23-27, 32.

continued there until ca. AD. 230-231. Therefore, the information that he imparts regarding the Synoptic Gospels is from a man not only of great learning and research but also one who was widely traveled.

Eusebius records the following from Origen's *Commentary on the Gospel of Matthew*:

> But in the first of his [*Commentaries*] on the *Gospel According to Matthew*, defending the canon of the Church, he gives his testimony that he knows only four Gospels, writing somewhat as follows: ". . . as having learnt by tradition concerning the four Gospels, which alone are unquestionable in the Church of God under heaven, that first was written that according to Matthew, who was once a tax-collector but afterwards an apostle of Jesus Christ, who published it for those who from Judaism came to believe, composed as it was in the Hebrew language. Secondly, that according to Mark, who wrote it in accordance with Peter's instructions, whom also Peter acknowledged as his son in the catholic epistle. . . . And thirdly, that according to Luke, who wrote, for those who from the Gentiles [came to believe], the Gospel that was the praise of Paul. After them all, that according to John.[98]

Here Origen's statement reflects an order of Matthew, Mark, Luke, and John, but nothing in the context requires this to be an assumed chronological order for Mark and Luke. His explicit statement is that Matthew wrote first and John last, but otherwise Eusebius' discussion centers in Origen's view of the exact number of the gospels

---

[98] Ibid., 6.25.3-6.

rather than in the order of their composition.[99] Most likely, Eusebius included Origen's statement because of its bearing on the *number* (not the *order*) of gospels in the canon of the church. He probably accepted Origen's order as reflecting the *canonical* order of appearance in NT manuscripts. On the other hand, Eusebius included Clement's statement cited earlier in this chapter because it related directly to the *chronological* sequence of composition of the gospels (i.e., Matthew, Luke, Mark, and John).[100]

In another place, Origen stressed the apostolic origin of the four gospels and rejected numerous apocryphal gospels as spurious. Origen accepted only four gospels: "For Matthew did not 'take in hand' but wrote by the Holy Spirit, and so did Mark and John and also equally Luke."[101] In this quotation, he does not distinguish between Greek and Aramaic versions of Matthew but includes the Greek Matthew as written by the apostle himself along with the other three gospels (i.e., John, Mark, and Luke). Though he was aware that Matthew originally wrote in Hebrew (see earlier quotation from his *Commentary on the Gospel of Matthew*), this latter statement implies that he made no distinction between the Aramaic and Greek versions but included the Greek as equally authoritative with the other three gospels and also stressed its origin from the Holy Spirit.

Just as with Tertullian and Clement, to doubt Origen's assertions that Matthew and John were written by apostles and that men associated with the apostles wrote the gospels that bear their names (i.e., Luke and Mark) would

---

[99] The larger context deals with Origen's view of the number of sacred writings in the OT and NT (ibid., 6.25.1-14).

[100] Farmer, "Patristic Evidence Reexamined," 14.

[101] Origen *Homily in Luke* I; cf. also Orchard and Riley, *Order of the Synoptics*, 137.

be to repudiate Origen's intelligence as a preeminent, careful scholar and also to question his integrity.

EUSEBIUS

Eusebius of Caesarea (ca. A.D. 260-ca. 340), bishop of Caesarea in Palestine, was a pupil of the presbyter Pamphilus, who was himself a student of Origen. Many look to him as the Father of Church History, especially in light of his most famous work *Ecclesiastical History*, which surveyed the history of the church from apostolic times until A.D. 324.[102] His purpose was to compose a record of past trials of the church at the end of its long struggle and the beginning of its era of prosperity. The work is particularly valuable since Eusebius had access to the excellent library housed at Caesarea and also the imperial archives. He also records that he exerted great effort, to be honest and objective in using the best and most reliable of the primary sources available to him.[103] Therefore, in many respects, Eusebius is an invaluable source of knowledge concerning the history of the church during her first three centuries of existence. Eusebius was also a participant in the Council of Nicaea (A.D. 325).

Much of the earlier information in this chapter has come from Eusebius' *Ecclesiastical History*. Much of *Ecclesiastical History* is a record of what others said and did, but at times, Eusebius appears to give his own personal views. He mentions that only two apostles, Matthew, and John, left their recollections and that they wrote under the pressure of necessity: "[T]hey took to

---

[102] *Ecclesiastical History* consists of ten books, the first seven of which recount the history of the church from the beginning to A.D. 303 and the last three some events in Eusebius's own lifetime until the Council of Nicaea in A.D. 325. He wrote in a strict chronological order.

[103] Eusebius *Ecclesiastical History* 1.1.1-8

writing perforce."[104] Though he mentions that Matthew first wrote in the Hebrew language, he also considers Greek Matthew to have come from the apostle's hand.[105] He notes that John was aware of Matthew, Mark, and Luke, and confirmed their accuracy when he composed his gospel.[106] He refers to sections of the Greek Matthew and ascribes them to the apostle as their author.[107]

In addition, according to Eusebius, Mark composed his gospel on the basis of Peter's preaching,[108] while Luke's gospel came about through his association "with Paul and his [Luke's] conversation with other apostles."[109]

AUGUSTINE

Augustine (ca. A.D. 354-430) was a younger contemporary of Jerome, who while young, studied grammar, Latin classics, and rhetoric with parental hopes for his becoming a lawyer or a high civil servant in the imperial government. After his conversion, he became a priest in A.D. 391 and in A.D. 396 the bishop of Hippo in North Africa. Some have acclaimed him as the greatest of the church fathers.[110] He left over one hundred books, five hundred sermons, and two hundred letters. His influence became pervasive not only in the African church but in the

---

[104] Ibid., 3.24.6

[105] Ibid., 3.24.5-7

[106] Ibid., 3.24.7-8

[107] Ibid., 3.24.9-10

[108] Ibid., 2.15.1-2

[109] Ibid., 3.24.15

[110] Augustine's *Confessions* 1-10 give the story of his life until shortly after his conversion. He gives an account of his conversion in 8.12.

Western Church, even surpassing that of Jerome. His most widely known work is probably his *Confessions*, one of the great autobiographical works of all time. His *City of God* may be his greatest apologetic work. He also wrote many other significant works including *The Harmony of the Gospels* and *Christian Doctrine*.

Augustine's position on the order of gospels composition appears in his *Harmony of the Gospels*: "Now, these four evangelists . . . are believed to have written in the order which follows: first Matthew, then Mark, thirdly Luke, lastly John."[111] Augustine here passes on a tradition of the order of composition as in the present NT canon. His assignment of Matthew as first and John as last is in overall harmony with earlier tradition as reviewed above in this chapter.

Yet, the Augustinian order conflicts with Clement's sequence in reversing the order of Mark and Luke. Militating against assigning too much weight to the aspect of Augustine's order of Mark being prior to Luke is that he, in contrast to Clement, does not clearly identify the origin of his information or show how widespread or general was the acceptance of his sequence. He merely states that they "are believed to have written in the order which follows." Significant questions remain unanswered as to who held the views he espouses, how widespread was the belief, and what evidence was available for the information he imparts.

In contrast, Clement's information has better documentation, for it is much earlier, reaching back into the early part of the second century and reflecting a widespread consensus. Augustine's is much later and unspecified as to source. Overall, such factors make

---

[111] Augustine *The Harmony of the Gospels* 1.2.3. Quotations from Augustine's *Harmony* come from Philip Schaff, ed., vol. 6 of *The Nicene and Post-Nicene Fathers*, here after designated *NPNF*.

Clement's information decidedly more weighty in molding a decision regarding the order of composition of the synoptics.

Within the same context, Augustine continues,

[A]s respects the task of composing that record of the gospel which is to be accepted as ordained by divine authority, there were (only) two, belonging to the number of those whom the Lord chose before the Passover, that obtained places,—namely, the first place and the last. For the first place in order was held by Matthew and the last by John. And thus the remaining two, who did not belong to the number referred to, but who at the same time had become followers of the Christ who spoke in those others, were supported on either side by the same, like sons who were to be embraced, and who in this way were set in the midst between these twain.[112]

Here Augustine implicitly accepts that the Greek Matthew came from the apostle Matthew as its author and that John was written by the apostle John. This latter quotation, however, appears most likely to deal with the order of the gospels within the canon and is not necessarily helpful for giving the order of composition. Neither does it specify whether Luke was prior to Mark or Mark prior to Luke.[113]

Augustine goes on to note that prior to the Greek version of Matthew the Apostle wrote first in the Hebrew language, once again confirming the tradition set forth by the other church fathers: "Of these four, it is true, only Matthew is reckoned to have written in the Hebrew

---

[112] Ibid.

[113] Cf. David Peabody, "Augustine and the Augustinian Hypothesis: A Reexamination of Augustine's Thought in De Consensu Evangelistarum," in *New Synoptic Studies*, William R. Farmer, ed. (Macon, Ga.: Mercer, 1983), 38.

language; the others in Greek." Yet as with other church fathers, he does not explain the transition from Aramaic to Greek but accepts without question that the Greek version was from the apostle.[114] He confirmed that latter point by following up his comments on the order of the gospels and on Matthew's composition of his gospel in Greek before the others with his analysis of the Greek Matthew (as well as the other Greek gospels) as to their themes and character, thereby leaving the strong impression that he saw no significant difference between the Aramaic and Greek versions of Matthew's gospel.[115]

At another place, Augustine commented that "Mark follows him [i.e. Matthew] closely and looks like his attendant and epitomizer."[116] That statement, however, appears not to be based on tradition but on Augustine's personal analysis of Matthew in comparison with Mark. Hence, no reveal significance attaches to it beyond the fact of reflecting Augustine's personal reflections and observations in explaining agreements between Matthew and Mark. Moreover, as the next section of this chapter will reveal, the church fathers viewed the gospels as being composed independently of one another. Augustine's *Harmony of the Gospels* evidences no indications to the contrary. As a matter of fact, it indicates just the opposite.

At another place, Augustine discusses the canonical order as follows:

> Now the whole canon of Scripture on which we say this judgment is to be exercised, is

---

[114] Augustine *The Harmony of the Gospels* 1.2.4. Augustine refers to the Hebrew Matthew at least two other times in his Harmony (2.66.128 and 2.80.157), in both of which places he refers to or quotes the Greek Matthew while talking about a Hebrew original. He never denies that the Greek version came from Matthew himself.

[115] Ibid., 1.2.5-6

[116] Ibid., 1.2.4.

contained in the following books. . . . That of the New Testament, again, is contained within the following:—Four books of the Gospel, according to Matthew, according to Mark, according to Luke, according to John.[117]

Here again he apparently reflects the compositional order of Matthew, Mark, Luke and John.

One other place deserves mention as possibly significant, for Augustine relates the following distinguishing characteristics of the contents of the gospels:

[I]t is a clearly admitted position that the first three—namely, Matthew, Mark and Luke—have occupied themselves chiefly with the humanity of our Lord Jesus Christ. . . . And in this way, Mark . . . either appears to be preferentially the companion of Matthew . . . or else, in accordance with the more probable account of the matter, he holds a course in conjunction with both [the other synoptists]. For although he is at one with Matthew in a large number of passages, he is nevertheless at one rather with Luke in some others.[118]

Peabody, who favors the Two Gospel Hypothesis, argues from this statement that Augustine has changed his mind regarding his relegation of Luke to third position in order of composition, reasoning that after Augustine's extensive analysis of the gospels "Augustine's new, more probable view of Mark is that Mark is literally dependent upon both Matthew and Luke" and "Augustine had not one but two views of the relationships among the

---

[117] Ibid., 2.8.13.

[118] Ibid., 4.10.11

Gospels."119 That conclusion is not warranted, however. Peabody has a strong desire to explain away the apparent Augustinian order of composition of Matthew, Mark, Luke, and John in hopes of establishing him as supportive of the Two-Gospel Hypothesis and its order of Matthew, Luke, Mark, and John. As a result, he reads too much into Augustine's statement. Augustine, in context, is merely describing the similarities and differences between the Gospel of John and the three Synoptic Gospels. Furthermore, in the immediate context, he refers to the gospels in the order Matthew, Mark, and Luke, thus giving a strong indication that he has not changed his mind regarding his assumed order of composition. Another explanation for Augustine's assertions is that he may have identified any established canonical order (Matthew, Mark, Luke, and John) with the order of composition, but demonstrating that beyond a reasonable doubt is impossible.

Above all, one point is important. Regardless of the difference of opinion between Clement and Augustine on the order of composition of the gospels, neither Augustine nor Clement place Mark first in order of composition as the Two-Document Theory supposes. Virtually *all* church fathers place Matthew earliest. Although they may mention a Hebrew or Aramaic original of Matthew, the fathers accepted without any serious question that the Greek Matthew came from the apostle Matthew, the Gospel of Luke from Luke's association with Paul, Mark from his association with Peter's preaching, and the apostle John's Gospel came last in order of composition.

CONCLUSION REGARDING ORDER OF COMPOSITION

An analysis of data from the church fathers results in one conspicuous conclusion: they do not support either

---

[119] Peabody, "Augustine and the Augustinian Hypothesis," 61-62.

the Two-Document Hypothesis or the Two-Gospel Hypothesis. The assumed dependence of Matthew and Luke on Mark is totally without historical foundation as is the assumed dependence of Mark on Matthew and Luke instead of on Peter's preaching. Strained and desperate interpretations by proponents of the Two-Document Hypothesis as well as by those of the Two-Gospel Hypothesis stand as a monumental testimony to their dismal failure in mustering any support among the fathers.

Papias' testimony answers the question as to whether Mark was in any sense dependent on Matthew as the Two-Gospel Theory would require, for Mark wrote on the basis of Peter's preaching, not on the basis of literary dependence on Matthew. Besides, the church fathers were not merely unthinkingly reflecting Papias, because they (e.g., Irenaeus, Clement, Tertullian, Origen) were renowned scholars in their own right who had information from widespread and independent sources. They did not need to rely solely on Papias for their information.

A newly released work, *Mark*, vol. II from the Ancient Christian Commentary on Scripture buttresses these contentions. This work, by appealing to the ancients, circumnavigates such sacrosanct, as well as highly erroneous, historical-critically cherished icons originating out of source, form, tradition and redaction criticism, revealing some interesting contradictions with post-Enlightenment assertions. For instance, the volume on Mark reveals that the early church fathers overwhelmingly neglected Mark, rarely produced a sustained commentary on Mark. Instead, Matthew and John received the most attention. While one could argue that they held Matthew and John in high esteem because they were apostolic, one still wonders why, if Mark was really the first written gospel as so ardently maintained by source criticism (contra the Two-Document Hypothesis), did the fathers so persistently neglect it. Moreover, the volume also reveals that the fathers consistently maintained that Mark actually wrote Mark (not some unknown "evangelist" as maintained by historical criticism) and that it reflected Peter's preaching rather than being a condensation of Matthew and Luke (contra the Two-Gospel Hypothesis). The conclusion the work reaches is astoundingly refreshing: "It had always been evident that Mark presented a shorter a shorter version of the gospel than Matthew, but the premise of literary dependency was not generally recognized. The view that Matthew and Luke directly relied on Mark did not develop in full form until the nineteenth century,"[120] Such a perspective also indicates that the fathers regarded Matthew, not Mark, as the first gospel to be written. From this reviewer's perspective, only by *a priori* reading into the church fathers of these two recent synoptic hypotheses move from acute speculation to enslaving dogma.

Far from contradicting each other, the information that these fathers supply is largely complementary, consistent, and congruent: the apostle Matthew wrote first, the apostle John last, with Luke and Mark writing between these two. Some difference of opinion exists as to whether Luke or Mark wrote second, but the probability is on the side of Luke's being second. Mark derived his material from the preaching of Peter, not from Matthew and Luke.

Sadly, the overarching reason why modern scholarship rejects or explains away their testimony is adherence to an assumed hypothesis of literary dependence, which is the basic assumption of Historical Criticism (hereafter HC). The church fathers stand solidly against the stultifying dogma of modern Source Criticism that blindly upholds the Two- (or Four-) Document Hypothesis and the Two-Gospel Hypothesis, theories that

---

[120] Thomas C. Oden & Christopher A. Hall, *Mark*, vol. II of Ancient Christian Commentary on Scripture (Downers Grove, IL: InterVarsity, 1998), xxix.

suppress, dismiss, or ridicule any evidence contrary their assumed tenets. Instead of being blindly rejected, explained away, or enervated by a pre-conceived agenda or predilection toward a particular synoptic hypothesis, the statements of the fathers should have their full weight in any discussion of the synoptic issue. Their voices objectively analyzed constitute a united witness against the concept of the priority of Mark based on literary dependence, and in turn, provide a cogent testimony for the chronological priority of the writing of Matthew. Could it be that Enlightenment-spawned historical-criticism has so systematically ignored the early fathers because they stand as manifest contradictions to its cherished dogmas or might it also reflect intellectual arrogance displayed by much of modern scholarship?

Bibliography

Arndt, William, Frederick W. Danker, and Walter Bauer. *A Greek-English Lexicon of the New Testament and Other Early Christian Literature. 3rd ed.* . Chicago: University of Chicago Press, 2000.

Black, Matthew. *"The Gospel of Matthew," in Studies in the Gospels and Epistles.* Manchester: Manchester University, 1962.

Campenhausen, Hans von. *The Formation of the Christian Bible.* Philadelphia: Fortress, 1972.

Carson, D. A., Douglas J. Moo, and Leon Morris. *An Introduction to the New Testament.* Grand Rapids: Zondervan, 1992.

Cruse, C. F. *Eusebius' Eccliatical History.* Peabody, MA: Hendrickson, 1998.

Filson, Floyd. *A Commentary on the Gospel According to Matthew, 2nd ed.* London: Adam & Charles Black, 1971.

France, R. T. *The Gospel According to Matthew: An Introduction and Commentary (Tyndale New Testament Commentaries).* Grand Rapids: Eerdmans, 1985.

Gundry, Robert H. *The Use of the Old Testament in St. Matthew's Gospel.* Leiden: E. J. Brill, 1967.

Harrison, Everett F. *Introduction to the New Testament.* Grand Rapids: Eerdmans, 1971.

Hiebert, D. Edmond. *An Introduction to the New Testament: Three Volume Collection.* Winona Lake, IN: BMH Books, 2003.

Hill, David. *The Gospel of Matthew, in The New Century Bible Commentary.* Grand Rapids: Eerdmans, 1972.

Liddell, Henry George et al.,. *A Greek-English Lexicon .* Oxford: Clarendon Press, 1996.

Louw, Johannes P, and Eugene Albert Nida. *Greek-English Lexicon of the New Testament : Based on Semantic Domains, 2nd edition.* New York: United Bible Societies, 1996.

Manson, T. W. *The Sayings of Jesus.* London: SCM Press, 1949.

—. *The Teaching of Jesus.* London: SCM Press, 1957.

Martin, Ralph P. *New Testament Foundations, vol. 1 of The Four Gospels.* Grand Rapids: Eerdmans, 1975.

Massaux, Édouard. *The Influence of the Gospel of Saint Matthew on Christian Literature Before Saint Irenaeus, trans. by Norman J. Belval and Suzanne Hecht, Arthur J. Bellinzoni, ed., 3 vols.* Macon, Georgia: Mercer University, 1993.

Nineham, D. E. *St. Mark.* Philadelphia: Westminster, 1963.

Oden, Thomas C., and Christopher A. Hall Mark. *vol. II of Ancient Christian Commentary on Scripture.* Downers Grove, IL: InterVarsity, 1998.

Stather Hunt, B. P. W. *Primitive Gospel Sources.* London: James Clarke & Co.,, 1951.

Walker, Williston, Richard A. Norris, David W. Lotz, and Robert T. Handy. *A History of the Christian Church, 4th ed.* New York: Charles Scribner's Sons, 1985.

www.ingramcontent.com/pod-product-compliance
Lightning Source LLC
Chambersburg PA
CBHW061344040426
42444CB00011B/3086